Have You Felt Like Giving Up Lately ?

Have You Felt Like Giving Up Lately?

David Wilkerson

Fleming H. Revell Company
Old Tappan, New Jersey

Scripture quotations are from the King James Version of the Bible.

Library of Congress Cataloging in Publication Data

Wilkerson, David R
  Have you felt like giving up lately?

  1. Christian life—1960-   I. Title.
BV4501.2.W5198   248.4   80-10402
ISBN 0-8007-5042-X

Contents

Foreword

This book has been in the making for years. It was born from a cry, deep in my heart, to help hurting people.

I travel, preaching crusades, across this great land; and I meet so many hurting people who can't seem to find relief from their problems. These hurting people are often divorced or separated. Some are lonely young people who can't find love. Others are caught in a web of despair, suffering from guilt, condemnation, depression, and fear.

It is my firm conviction that, in one way or another, we are all hurting. We all need healing of our inner hurts. We need to know how to get hold of a genuine peace and a true freedom from the bondage of besetting sins. It is sin that causes so many of our problems and hurts.

I hope this book will help multitudes of Christians find true healing. Already, a great number of friends have been healed as a result of the messages included here.

Healing is a process. Read every chapter and witness that powerful healing process take place in your life. I can say that with boldness, because I know these messages were born in prayer, bathed in tears, tested through personal sorrow and suffering, and, most important of all, founded on the true Word of God.

Have You Felt Like Giving Up Lately ?

1

When You Hurt

In one way or another, we are all hurting. Everyone is in the same boat. Even the laughing, happy-go-lucky crowd is hurting. They try to hide their hurt by drinking and joking, but it won't go away.

Who hurts? The parents of a prodigal son or daughter. Millions of parents have been deeply wounded by children who have rejected their counsel. Those loving parents grieve over the deception and delinquency of children who were once tender and good.

The victims of broken homes are hurting. The abandoned wife whose husband rejected her for another woman is hurting. The husband who lost the love of a wife is hurting. The children who lost their security are hurting.

Others suffer illness: cancer, heart problems, and a myriad of other human diseases. To be told by a doctor, "You have cancer; you may die!" has to be terrifying. Yet many reading this message have experienced such pain and agony.

Lovers break up. A boyfriend or girlfriend walks away, trampling on what was once a beautiful relationship. All that is left is a broken, wounded heart.

And what about the unemployed? The despondent ones whose dreams have collapsed? The shut-ins? The prisoners? The homosexuals? The alcoholics?

It is true! In one way or another we are all hurting. Every person on earth carries his own burden of pain and hurt.

There Is No Physical Cure

When you are deeply hurt, no person on this earth can shut out the innermost fears and deepest agonies. The best of friends cannot really understand the battle you are going through or the wounds inflicted on you.

Only God can shut out the waves of depression and feelings of loneliness and failure which come over you. Faith in God's love alone can salvage the hurt mind. The bruised and broken heart that suffers in silence can be healed only by a supernatural work of the Holy Spirit, and nothing short of divine intervention really works.

God has to step in and take over. He has to intercept our lives at the breaking point, stretch forth His loving arms, and bring that hurting body and mind under His protection and care. God must come forth as a caring Father and demonstrate that He is there, making things turn out for good. He must, by His own power, dispel the storm clouds, chase away the despair and gloom, wipe away the tears, and replace the sorrow with peace of mind.

Why Me, Lord?

What hurts most is that you know your love for God is strong, yet you can't seem to understand what He is trying to work out in your life. If you were cold toward His love, you could understand why prayers went unanswered. If you were running from God, you could probably understand why the testings and severe trials kept coming on. If you were a down-and-out sinner, who despised the things of God, you could bring yourself to believe you deserved to be hurt badly. But you are not running; you are not rejecting Him in any way. You long to do His perfect will. You yearn to please God and want only to serve Him with all that is in you. That is why your hurting is so debilitating. It makes you feel there is something terribly wrong with you. You question your spiritual depth, and at times, you even question your sanity. From somewhere deep inside you, a voice whispers, "Maybe I'm defective, somehow. Maybe I'm being hurt so deeply because God can't see much good in me. I must be so out of His will; He has to discipline me to make me obedient."

Friends Try So Hard to Help

A bruised or broken heart causes the most excruciating pain known to mankind. Most other human hurts are only physical, but a heart that is wounded must carry a pain that is both physical and spiritual. Friends and loved ones can help soothe the physical pain of a broken heart. When they are there, laughing, loving, and caring, the physical pain eases, and there is temporary relief. But night falls, and with it comes the terror of spiritual agony. Pain is always worse in the night. Loneliness falls like a cloud, when the sun disappears. The hurting explodes when you are all alone, trying to understand how to cope with the inner voices and fears that keep surfacing.

Your friends, who really don't understand what you are going through, offer all kinds of easy solutions. They get impatient with you. They are mostly happy and carefree, at the time; and they can't understand why you don't simply snap out of it. They suspect you are indulging in self-pity. They remind you the world is filled with heartbroken, hurting people who have survived. More often, they want to pray that one-time, cure-all, solve-everything prayer. You are told to "release your faith, claim a promise, confess a cure, and walk away from your despair."

That's all well and good, but it's preaching that usually comes from Christians who have never known much suffering in their own lives. They are like Job's baby-sitters, who knew all the answers but who could not relieve his pain. Job said to them, ". . . ye are all physicians of no value" (Job 13:4). Thank God for well-meaning friends, but if they could experience your agony for even one hour, they would be changing their tunes. Put them in your place just once, feeling what you feel, experiencing the inner pain you carry, and they would be saying to you, "How in the world can you take it? I couldn't handle what you are going through!"

Time Heals Nothing

Then there is that age-old cliché, "Time heals all wounds." You are told to hang in there, put on a smile, and wait for time to anesthetize your pain. But I suspect all the rules and clichés about loneliness are coined by happy, unhurt people. It sounds good, but it is not true. Time heals nothing; only God heals!

When you are hurting, time only magnifies the pain. Days and weeks go by, and the agony hangs on. The hurting won't go away, no matter what the calendar says. Time may push the pain deeper into the mind, but one tiny memory can bring it to the surface.

Truthfully, it doesn't help much, either, to know Christians have suffered before you down through the ages. You can identify with the suffering of Bible characters who survived tremendous ordeals of pain. But knowing that others have gone through great battles doesn't calm the hurt in your own bosom. When you read how they victoriously came out of their battles, and you still haven't, it only adds to your hurt. It makes you feel as though they were very close to God to receive such answers to their prayers. It makes you feel unworthy of the Lord, because your problem lingers on, in spite of all your spiritual efforts.

Double Trouble

People seldom get hurt just once. Most who hurt can show you other wounds also. Pain is layered over pain. A broken heart is usually a tender, fragile one. It is easily broken because it is not protected by a hard shell. Tenderness is mistaken for vulnerability, by the hard-shelled heart. Quietness is misjudged as a weakness. A total giving of oneself to another is mistaken as coming on too strong. The heart that is not afraid to admit its need of love is misjudged as being too sexually oriented.

It follows then that a tender heart which reaches for love and understanding is often the easiest to break. Hearts that are open and trusting are usually the ones that are wounded the most. This world is filled with men and women who have rejected the love offered to them from a heart that is gentle and tender. Those strong, hard-shelled hearts that trust no one, hearts that give so little, hearts that demand love be constantly proved, hearts that are always calculating, hearts that are always manipulating and self-serving, hearts that are afraid to risk are the ones that seldom get broken. They don't get wounded, because there is nothing to wound. They are too proud and self-centered to allow anyone else to make them suffer in any way. They go about breaking other hearts and trampling on the fragile souls who touch their lives, simply because they are so thick and dull at heart themselves, and they think everyone should be just as they are. The hard hearts don't like tears. They hate commitment. They feel smothered when asked to share from their own hearts.

Heartbreakers Do Not Get Off Easy

Part of the pain a broken heart must suffer is the thought that the offender, the heartbreaker, is going to get away with it all. The heart says, "I am the one hurt and wounded; yet I'm the one who pays the price. The offender gets off scot-free, when he should pay for what he did." That's the problem with crosses; the wrong person usually gets crucified. But God keeps the books, and on Judgment Day, the books will be balanced. But even in this life, heartbreakers and people wounders pay a high price. No matter how they try to justify their hurtful actions, they cannot drown out the cries of the ones they have wounded. Like the blood of Abel, which cried out from the ground, the cries of a broken heart can pierce the barrier of time and space and terrorize the hardest of hearts. Hurts are usually caused by outright lies, and every liar must eventually be brought to justice.

Is there a balm for a broken heart? Is there healing for those deep, inner hurts? Can the pieces be put back together and the heart be made even stronger? Can the person who has known such horrible pain and suffering rise out of the ashes of depression and find a new and more powerful way of life? Yes! Absolutely yes! And if not, then God's Word would be a hoax, and God Himself would be a liar. That cannot be!

Let me share a few simple thoughts about how to cope with your hurt.

Stop trying to figure out how and why you got hurt. What has happened to you is a very common ailment among mankind. Your situation is not unique at all. It is the way of human nature. Whether you were right or wrong means absolutely nothing at this point. All that matters now is your willingness to move on in God and trust His mysterious workings in your life. The Bible says:

> . . . think it not strange concerning the fiery trial which is to try you, as though some strange thing happened unto you: But rejoice, inasmuch as ye are partakers of Christ's sufferings; that, when his glory shall be revealed, yet may be glad also with exceeding joy.
>
> 1 Peter 4:12, 13

God didn't promise to give you a painless way of life: He promised you a way of escape. He promised you help to bear your pain and to give you strength to put you back on your feet when weakness makes you stagger.

Most likely you did what you had to do. You moved in the will of God, honestly following your heart. You went into it with an open heart, willing to give of yourself. Love was your motivation. You did not abort the will of God; someone else did. If that were not true, you would not be the one who is hurting so. You are hurt because you tried to be honest.

You can't understand why things blew up in your face, when God seemed to be leading all along. Your heart asks, "Why did God allow me to get into this in the first place, if He knew it would never work out right?" But the answer is clear. Judas was called by the Lord; he was destined to be a man of God. He was handpicked by the Saviour; he could have been mightily used by God. But Judas aborted God's plan. He broke the heart of Jesus. What started out as a beautiful, perfect plan of God ended in disaster, because Judas chose to go his own way. Pride and stubbornness wrecked the plan of God that was in operation.

So lay off all your guilt trips. Stop condemning yourself. Stop trying to figure out what you did wrong. It is what you are thinking right now that really counts with God. You did not make a mistake; more than likely, you simply gave too much. Like Paul, you have to say, "The more I loved, the less I was loved"(*see* 2 Corinthians 12:15).

Remind yourself God knows exactly how much you can take, and He will not permit you to reach a breaking point. Our loving Father said:

> There hath no temptation taken you but such as is common to man: but God is faithful, who will not suffer you to be tempted above that ye are able; but will with

the temptation also make a way to escape, that ye may be
able to bear it.

1 Corinthians 10:13

The worst kind of blasphemy is to think God is behind all
your hurt and pain, that it is the heavenly Father disciplining
you, that God thinks you need one or two more heartbreaks
before you are ready to receive His blessings. Not so!

It is true the Lord chastens those He loves. But that chas-
tening is only for a season and is not meant to hurt us. God is
not the author of the confusion in your life; neither are you. It
is human failure. It is the enemy sowing tares in your field of
endeavor. It is the deception in someone else near you, who
lost faith in God. The enemy tries to hurt us through other
humans, just as he tried to hurt Job through an unbelieving
wife.

Your heavenly Father watches over you with an unwaver-
ing eye. Every move is monitored. Every tear is bottled. He
identifies with your every pain. He feels every hurt. He
knows when you have been exposed to enough harassment
from the enemy. He steps in and says, "Enough!" When the
hurt and pain no longer draw you closer to the Lord, when,
instead, it begins to downgrade your spiritual life, God moves
in. He will not permit a trusting child of His to go under
because of too much pain and agony of soul. When the hurting
begins to work to your disadvantage, when it begins to hinder
your growth, God must act and lift you out of the battle for a
while. He will never allow you to drown in your tears. He will
not permit your hurt to destroy your mind. He promises to
come, right on time, to wipe away your tears and give you joy
for mourning. God's word says: ". . . weeping may endure for
a night, but joy cometh in the morning" (Psalms 30:5).

**When you hurt the worst, go to your secret prayer closet and
weep out all your bitterness.**   Jesus wept. Peter wept bit-
terly! Peter carried with him the hurt of denying the very Son

of God. He walked alone on the mountains, weeping in sorrow. Those bitter tears worked a sweet miracle in him. He came back to shake the kingdom of Satan.

A woman who had endured a mastectomy wrote a book entitled *First You Cry*. How true! Recently I talked with a friend who was just informed he had terminal cancer. "The first thing you do," he said, "is cry until there are no more tears left. Then you begin to move closer to Jesus, until you know His arms are holding you tight."

Jesus never looks away from a crying heart. He said, "A broken heart will I not despise" (*see* Psalms 51:17). Not once will the Lord say, "Get hold of yourself! Stand up and take your medicine! Grit your teeth and dry your tears." No! Jesus bottles every tear in His eternal container.

Do you hurt? Bad? Then go ahead and cry! And keep on crying until the tears stop flowing. But let those tears originate only from hurt, and not from unbelief or self-pity.

Convince yourself you will survive, you will come out of it; live or die, you belong to the Lord. Life does go on. You would be surprised how much you can bear, with God helping you. Happiness is not living without pain or hurt—not at all. True happiness is learning how to live one day at a time, in spite of all the sorrow and pain. It is learning how to rejoice in the Lord, no matter what has happened in the past.

You may feel rejected. You may feel abandoned. Your faith may be weak. You may think you are down for the count. Sorrow, tears, pain, and emptiness may swallow you up, at times; but God is still on His throne. He is still God!

You can't help yourself. You can't stop the pain and hurt. But our blessed Lord will come to you, and He will place His loving hand under you and lift you up to sit again in heavenly places. He will deliver you from the fear of dying. He will reveal His endless love for you.

Look up! Encourage yourself in the Lord. When the fog

surrounds you and you can't see any way out of your dilemma, lie back in the arms of Jesus and simply trust Him. He has to do it all! He wants your faith, your confidence. He wants you to cry aloud, "Jesus loves me! He is with me! He will not fail me! He is working it all out, right now! I will not be cast down! I will not be defeated! I will not be a victim of Satan! I will not lose my mind or my direction! God is on my side! I love Him and He loves me!"

The bottom line is faith. And faith rests on this one absolute: "No weapon that is formed against thee shall prosper . . ." (Isaiah 54:17).

2

You Can't Carry
Your Own Cross

It's very true that Jesus said to His disciples, ". . . If any man will come after me, let him deny himself, and take up his cross, and follow me" (Matthew 16:24). But Jesus could not carry His cross, and neither can you! Jesus fell under the load of His cross, weary, exhausted, and unable to carry it another step. John said, "And he bearing his cross went forth into a place called . . . Golgotha" (John 19:17). The Bible doesn't tell us how far Jesus carried His cross. We do know Simon of Cryrene was compelled to pick it up and carry it to the place of crucifixion (Matthew 27:32).

Jesus did take up His cross and was led by His tormentors, like a lamb to be slain. But He could not carry it for long. The truth is, Jesus was too weak and frail to carry His cross. It was laid on another's shoulders. He had reached the end of His endurance; He was a physically broken and wounded man. There is only so much one person can take. There is a breaking point.

Why did they compel Simon to pick up that cross? Was Jesus lying on that cobblestone street, like a lifeless man, with the cross lying over Him like dead weight? Did they kick

Him, try to prop Him up, and attempt to force Him a step farther? And did He just lie there with not enough strength to move an inch? His cross had become too heavy to bear.

What does this mean to us? Would our Lord make us do something He could not do? Did He not say, "And whosoever doth not bear his cross, and come after me, cannot be my disciple"? (Luke 14:27). A cross is a cross, be it wooden or spiritual. It is not enough to say, "His cross was different; our cross is spiritual."

Personally, it gives me great hope to know Jesus could not take up His cross. It encourages me to know I am not the only one burdened down to the ground at times, unable to go on in my own strength. If we are going to identify with His crucifixion, we must also identify with the steps that led to the cross. We must face, once and for all, the truth that no human being can carry his own cross.

Don't look for some hidden interpretation; Jesus knew exactly what He was saying when He called us to take up our crosses and follow Him. He remembers His cross. He remembers that another had to carry it for Him. Why, then, would He ask us to shoulder crosses He knows will soon crush us to the ground? He knows we can't carry them all the way in our own strength. He knows all about the agony, the helplessness, and the burden a cross creates.

There is a truth hidden here which we must uncover. It is a truth so powerful and edifying, it could change the way we look at all our troubles and hurts. Even though it almost sounds sacrilegious to suggest Jesus did not carry His own cross, that is the truth. What it means to us today is that Jesus, who is touched by the feelings of our infirmities, must experience for Himself what it is like to be weak, discouraged, and unable to go on without help. He was in all points tempted just as we are. The temptation is not in failing or in laying down the cross because of weakness. The real temptation is in trying to pick up that cross and carrying it on in our own strength. God could have supernaturally lifted that cross and magically levitated it all the way to Calvary. Then, too, He could have taken the weight out of the cross and made it featherlike. But He did not. The crucifixion scene was not a series of blunders, and, though Christ died at the hands of sinners, the entire plan was borne in the heart of God from the foundation of the world. God put Simon there, ready to play his part in the plan of redemption. God was not caught by surprise when His Son could no longer carry the cross and thus fulfill prophecy. God knew Jesus would take up His cross, follow toward Golgotha, then lay it down.

Your Cross Is Meant to Bring You Down

God knows also that not one of His children can carry the cross he takes up when following Christ. We so much want to be good disciples; we so much want to deny ourselves and take the cross upon ourselves. We seem to forget that same cross will one day bring us to the end of our human strength and endurance. Would Jesus purposely ask us to take up crosses that He knows will sap all our human energies and leave us lying helpless—even to the point of giving up? Absolutely! Jesus forewarns us, ". . . without me ye can do nothing" (John 15:5). So He asks us to take up our crosses and struggle on with them, until we learn that lesson. Not until our crosses push us down into the dust, do we learn the lesson that it is not by our might nor power nor strength, but it is by His power. That is what the Bible means when it says His strength is made perfect in our weakness. It has never meant that God's way is a little better than ours or that His strength is a bit superior. It means that God's way is the only way; His strength is the only hope!

Jesus looks upon this world—filled with confused children

going about trying to establish their own righteousness and trying to please Him in their own ways—and He calls for crosses. The cross is meant to break us, to drain us of all human effort. We know we have One stronger than Simon who will come at our breaking point and take over the burden, but He cannot take over until we give up, until we come to that point where we cry, "God, I can't go another step. I'm exhausted! I'm broken! My strength is gone! I feel dead! Help!"

Jesus was crucified "through weakness" (2 Corinthians 13:4). It is when we become totally weak and self-abased that we witness the crucifixion of our own pride. Out of weakness we are made strong, by faith in the Lord. Our spirits are willing to carry our own crosses, but our flesh is weak. Paul could glory in his cross, taking pleasure in how weak it made him. He said:

> . . . I take pleasure in infirmities, in reproaches, in necessities, in persecutions, in distresses for Christ's sake: for when I am weak, then am I strong. And he said unto me, My grace is sufficient for thee: for my strength is made perfect in weakness. . . .
>
> 2 Corinthians 12:10,9

Paul was not weak and strong at the same time. He grew weak because of troubles and distresses. But when he was cast down to the ground by his cross, he did not despair. It was out of that weakness he became strong. Paul rejoiced in this process of being made weak, because it was the secret to his power with Christ. ". . . Most gladly therefore will I rather glory in my infirmities, that the power of Christ may rest upon me" (2 Corinthians 12:9).

What is your cross? It is any burden or pressure that threatens to break you down! My junkie friends call theirs "a monkey on the back." That is not a sacrilegious reference to the cross; it simply defines their image of a burden that crushes them to the ground. I have often heard husbands and wives refer to their marriages as their "cross to bear." Others see their cross as an unfulfilling job, an illness, a state of loneliness, or divorce. I have heard all kinds of definitions of what the cross is supposed to represent. I have even heard homosexuals refer to their habit as a heavy cross. Since Jesus did not describe the details of the cross we are to take up, I suggest it is anything that will hasten a crisis in our spiritual lives. For example, loneliness can be a cross, if it becomes a burden too heavy to bear and if it finally brings us to the end of ourselves. It is then we can allow the Lord to reach down to us and lift us out of our pity and self-destructiveness. Loneliness is a good thing, if it makes us weak enough to want only His strength.

"I'm not doing enough for God." My cross is peculiar, but not unfamiliar to many others. I am constantly burdened by a sense of *never doing enough.* This cross usually becomes the heaviest right after I've written a best-selling book, after I've preached to thousands, after I've launched a feeding program for starving children, or after I've counseled with hundreds of troubled couples. I stop for a few weeks, take inventory of my life and ministry, and something in me gets restless. I get depressed and confess to my wife and friends, "I don't feel as if I'm doing anything for God. I'm not as fulfilled as I should be. Sometimes I feel so useless."

So often I get that "unfinished" feeling. I feel I'm wasting too much time doing insignificant things. It's hard to relax when a voice inside condemns me for not "burning out for Jesus." I think of all the things I promise myself I will do, the projects I'll finish, the growth in God I'll achieve, and much of it never gets done. I accuse myself of being lazy. Others seem to be so disciplined and motivated, and I picture them, in my

mind, as passing me by, leaving me behind in the dust. But
God will ask me to keep taking up that cross daily, until it
finally gets the best of me. Evidently that's a part of my life
that is not yet under His control. One day I'll fall down in
despair and cry, "Lord, I just don't care anymore. Let the
world pass me by. Let my dreams all fade. Let me be nothing
but an obedient disciple. I don't want to compete with myself
or others anymore. No more ego goals. Take over, Lord, and
lift my load." That is when our Lord will step in and whisper,
"Now, David, let Me carry your load."

Spiritual crosses.   Sometimes spiritual pride can be a cross.
You take on a heavy load when you begin to testify about the
great things God is doing in your life. God gives you a broken
and contrite spirit; others come to you for help, and they
receive blessings; you are used in wonderful ways to encourage people all around you. It begins to dawn on you, "Wow!
I've had such great joy. God has made me so tender and
loving. I'm finally learning how to overcome my temptations,
and I'm growing so much in the Lord. I feel as if I'm about to
break through into a life of spiritual glory and power. At last
I've reached a place of trust and peace. I don't ever want to go
back to what I was."

A week later, you are groveling in the dust; your spiritual
balloon burst, and everything seems to have drained out of
you. All you can say is, "What happened? I haven't sinned
against God; I haven't doubted. The joy just disappeared. I
don't seem to have anything in me now to give to others. I'm
dry and empty. Why couldn't I have kept the beautiful feelings?"

You Will Never *Arrive*

Hear me, friend. God will never permit you to feel as if you
have arrived. That's the trouble with too many Christians

today. Way back, they received a great blessing from the Lord. God did a wonderful work in their lives. The Holy Spirit came upon them and redid their lives, through and through. It was glorious, and they started telling the world about their awakening. But it's been downhill ever since. They have been riding out that one great experience and, in the process, have become self-satisfied and complacent. Take heed when you think you stand, lest you fall. Finally, that once-blessed Christian ends up feeling weak and empty. After trying, unsuccessfully, to invest and recreate the blessings, he gives up in despair. He cries out, "I'm spiritually dead. I'm losing ground with God. I feel like a phony. I can't seem to get back to where I was in the Lord."

Your love for Jesus can put you on your knees, but your cross will put you on your face—on the ground, in the dust. God meets you in your prostrate condition and whispers, "I have chosen the weak things of the world; the foolish things; the broken things; the things that are nothing, that no flesh should glory in His presence."

The Cross Teaches Us How to Deny Self

We will have to carry our crosses until we learn to deny. Deny what? The one thing that constantly hinders God's work in our lives: self. Look again at what Jesus said: "If any man will come after me, let him deny himself, and take up his cross and follow me." We are misinterpreting this message if we emphasize self-denial, that is, the rejection of material or unlawful things. Jesus was not calling upon us to learn self-discipline before we take up our cross. It is far more severe than that. Jesus is asking that we deny ourselves. This means to deny our own ability to carry any cross in our own strength. In other words, "Don't take up your cross until you are ready to reject any and every thought of becoming a holy disciple as a result of your own effort."

There are millions of professing Christians who boast about their self-denial. They don't drink or smoke or curse or fornicate; they are examples of tremendous discipline. But not in a hundred years would they admit it was accomplished by anything other than their own willpower. In fact, they are quick to add statements like the following: "I can quit any time I want." "The devil can't trick me." "I know what's right and I try to do it." "I keep all the commandments." "I'm a clean, moral person." "I don't lie or cheat, and I am faithful to my marriage vows."

They are practicing self-denial, but they have never denied self. In some ways, we are all like that. We experience spurts of holiness, accompanied by feelings of purity. Good works usually produce good feelings. But God will not allow us to think our good works and clean habits can save us. That is why we need a cross.

I believe Jesus is actually saying to us, "Before you take up your cross, be ready to face a moment of truth. Be ready to experience a crisis by which you will learn to deny your self-will, your self-righteousness, your self-sufficiency, your self-authority. You can rise up and follow Me as a true disciple only when you can freely admit you can do nothing in your own strength. You cannot overcome sin through your own willpower. Your temptations cannot be overcome by your self-efforts alone. You cannot work things out by your own intellect."

Jesus Never Forces a Cross on Us

Jesus said, "Let *him* take up his cross." Never once does our Lord say, "Stoop down and let *Me* lay a cross on you." Jesus is not in the drafting business; His army is all volunteer. Not all Christians carry crosses. You can be a believer without carrying a cross, but you cannot be a disciple. I see so many believers rejecting the way of the cross. They have opted for the good life, with its prosperity, its material gain, its popularity and success. I'm sure many of them will make heaven— they will have saved their skins, but they will not have learned Christ. Having rejected the suffering and sorrow of the cross, they will not have the capacity to know and enjoy Him in eternity, as will all the cross-bearing saints who have entered into the fellowship of His suffering. Those who suffer will reign together.

I am not glorifying the suffering and pain—only the results they produce. Like Paul, we should look at the trials and hurts we are now experiencing and rejoice in the knowledge we are going down the only path that leads to ultimate victory and maturity. No longer, then, do we look at our burdens and troubles as accidents and penalties, but as crosses that are offered to teach us submission to God's way of doing things.

If you are hurting right now, you are in the process of healing. If you are down, crushed under the burden of a heavy load, get ready! God is about to show Himself strong on your behalf. You are at the point of revelation. At any time now, your Simon will appear, because God does use people to perform His will. Someone is going to be compelled by the Holy Spirit to come into your path of suffering, reach out to you, and help lift your burden.

Your Cross Is a Sign of His Love

Dear friend, don't think of your trial as judgment from God. Don't go about condemning yourself, as though you have brought down upon yourself some dreaded penalty for failure. Stop thinking, "God is making me pay for my sin." Why can't you see that what you are going through is a result of His love? Are you being chastened? Do you feel as if you are being dragged down? Are you in pain? Are you suffering? Good!

That is the evidence of His love toward you. Submit! Take up your cross! Be prepared to go down even more. Get ready to reach your crisis. Get ready to reach the end of yourself. Be prepared to give up. Be prepared to hit bottom!

Please understand you are in Christ's own school of discipleship. Rejoice that you are going to become weak in order to experience His overpowering strength in you.

He laid His cross down; why won't you? For Him, a Simon appeared. For us, a Saviour appears. We get up and go on. It's still our cross, but now it's on His shoulders.

> Two are better than one; because they have a good reward for their labour. For if they fall, the one will lift up his fellow: but woe to him that is alone when he falleth; for he hath not another to help him up.
>
> Ecclesiastes 4:9, 10

3

You Can't Depend on
Others for Your Happiness

Recently a sad young minister and his wife came to me for counseling. After four troubled years of marriage, and two children, they were contemplating divorce. She was the saddest-looking wife I have seen in years. Her husband, the young youth minister, stood nearby, shuffling his weight from foot to foot, while his teary-eyed wife sobbed out her confession to me.

"There is absolutely no hope for our marriage now," she cried. "We are in two different worlds. He is so wrapped up in his work; he has no time left for me and the children. My whole world has been wrapped up in him; but now I'm getting tired of sitting home, waiting for him. I'm not accomplishing anything on my own. I don't even know if I love him anymore."

It hurt me to see such a lovely young couple acting like strangers to each other. I recognized the cause of their problem immediately: Both were bored, restless, and unhappy with each other. Just as multitudes of other couples, they once stood before a minister, to be married; they were gazing lovingly into each other's eyes, with their hearts filled with hope and anticipation that their marriage would be happy and fulfilling. Now, just a few years later, their hopes are in ashes. They became disillusioned, and, try as they may, they can't seem to rekindle the spark of first love. It is then the ugly thoughts of divorce surface.

I looked that young wife in the eye and said, "What a shame that all your happiness depends only on what your husband does. If he is a good husband, if he treats you the way you think you should be treated, if he spends a little time with you—then you may find a little happiness. But when he lets you down, you have nothing left. Your whole world rises and falls on the actions of your husband. That is why you are so empty."

She nodded affirmatively, then bowed her head sheepishly while I continued. "Young lady, you're not a whole person. You're just half a person. You cannot survive if you depend on someone else for your happiness. True women's liberation means finding your own happiness, in yourself, through God's power. You must become your own person and quit depending on your husband, or someone else, to make you happy."

She knew I was right—I had hit the nail right on the head. She promised to change her way of thinking and get involved with life, herself. I left them, convinced she was determined to step out of her role as an emotional cripple and find her own source of happiness through a new relationship with God.

The True Cause of Divorce and Broken Relationships

Husbands and wives are becoming emotional cripples who lean all over each other, causing both to fall. We mess up our relationships because we live under the influence of a lie. We have convinced ourselves we have a right to happiness and that our spouses are morally obligated to create it for us. The danger of that lie is that when we can't find the happiness we expect from them, we put all the blame on their failure to do what was right.

Our divorce courts today are overcrowded with husbands and wives seeking divorce simply on the grounds that their marriage gives them no happiness. One such divorced husband told me, "God bless my dear wife; she tried so hard. I gave that woman three of the best years of my life, hoping she could learn to understand me and make me feel like a man. She just didn't have it in her. She simply did not know how to make me happy."

That man will probably get married once or twice again, hoping a new wife will succeed where the first one failed. Some keep marching down the aisle with one new partner after another, trying desperately to find one understanding soul mate who will create happiness for them. But they seldom find it. Their misery and unhappiness increase with each new marriage partner.

No other human being on earth can create happiness for you. You must create it for yourself through the work of God in your own life. Marriage is not made up of two halves trying to become a whole. Rather, marriage consists of two whole people who are bridged by the Spirit of God. Marriage never works unless each party maintains his or her own identity, settles his own values, finds his own sense of fulfillment, and discovers his own source of happiness. Each must be complete, in himself, through the Lord.

Why allow what someone else does to destroy your life? Why permit the actions of another to rob you of your peace and joy? Why can't you be your own person? Why can't you look life right in the eye and say, "From now on, I'll not allow someone else to drag me down. I am determined to be a whole person, and I will discover my own source of happiness. No more leaning on someone else to give meaning and purpose to my life! I want a happiness that will not be lost just because somebody fails me."

Step Out of Your Bondage to the Actions of Others

I say to every housewife who will hear me: "Step out of your bondage of living your life only through others." God never intended that you find happiness only through your husband or your children. I am not suggesting that you forsake them, only that you forsake your degrading bondage to the idea that your happiness depends only on other people. God wants you to discover a life of true happiness and contentment, based only on what you are as a person and not on the moods and whims of people around you.

Wives who become clinging vines are not attractive to intelligent men. Husbands eventually walk all over wives who lean on them and exude an attitude that suggests, "You are my whole world, and if you ever let me down, I might as well kill myself." Wives who become independently happy and content in and with themselves suddenly become mystifyingly attractive. The truly attractive wife is the one who can say to her husband, "I love you, and I'll be your friend, but I'm a person, too. I'm going to act like a whole person, and my happiness will be what I create through my own relationship with God."

This is also a message that every young person must heed to survive the pressures of broken relationships so common today. How can young people find happiness when their parents are splitting up and their homes are disintegrating? They, too, need to learn not to depend on others for their happiness.

A nineteen-year-old girl confessed, "My dad and mom have been in love for over twenty-three years. I think theirs is just about a perfect marriage. If I ever learned they had been having problems and were putting on a good front just for me, I think I'd die. In fact, if my folks ever got a divorce, I'd go out and do drugs, sex, and alcohol, just to get even with them. I'd throw my life away."

"What a horrible concept," I told her. "Isn't it a shame that all your happiness depends on what your parents do? If they fail, so does your purpose in life. You will go all through life substituting others in the place of your parents. You will always have to have an idol—someone to be your good example. You will never be your own person. You will fail only because someone else fails you. What a pity!"

Our young people today must learn to find their own sources of happiness; they must no longer depend on their parents to create it for them. Thank God I am now meeting hundreds of young people who have found their own places of happiness in the Lord. One young man told me, "I love my parents, but I'm not going to allow their divorce to affect me. I'm going on with God. I have my own life to live, and I'm not going to let them drag me down by their actions."

We must give ourselves to the needs of others. We must help heal the hurts of those we love. We must get under one another's burdens, but we can do all of this only when we are happy with ourselves. We can help others find themselves only after we have found ourselves in the Lord.

There Is a Right Way to Find Happiness

I'm not one who cares much for formulas or how-to directions. But in my own experience, I have found a simple way to find a true happiness that does not depend on what others do. It is a happiness that does not come and go, and it is not affected by the moods, words, or actions of people in my life—even those I love the most.

What is that secret? *I have discovered that my needs are spiritual, not physical!* Our basic human needs include food, water, shelter, and the air we breathe. Beyond that, our needs are spiritual. And those needs can't be met by any human being.

All unhappiness is a result of trying to meet our needs through human relationships. When another human being fails to meet our needs, we become frustrated and unhappy. For example, the husband comes home from work tired, short-tempered, and feeling a need for a kind, understanding word from his wife. He is depressed, and he wants his wife to make him feel better. In turn, his wife has her own needs. She is feeling down, lonely, and she is wanting him to lift her spirits. So they lean on each other. The unspoken message rings out, "I'm hurting, honey, heal me. I'm down, lift me up. I'm depressed, make me happy. I'm blue, take my blues away. I'm in need, meet that need. Put your arms around me and love all the hurt out of me."

Of course, neither of them can meet the needs in the other, because those needs are spiritual, and only God can meet them. You can be in the arms of someone you love all night long and still wake up crying inside. The discovery is soon made that those needs cannot be met by sex or by a tender word. That is why some men pay a prostitute one hundred dollars a night, just to sit up and talk with them. They hope their blues can be talked away. It never works, because the next night they are seeking someone else to share their problems with.

We expect our spouses to do Godlike work. We expect miracles of them. We know only that we have overwhelming needs and that they must be met.

I have had lonely people tell me, "If only God would give me someone to love, I'd be such a better person and a better Christian. I know all my unhappiness is a result of being so alone all the time. I need a friend; only then will I be truly happy."

I say, "Not so!" Another person, male or female, may give you temporary relief from the agony of loneliness; but, unless you are a whole person, with your own source of inner strength, the old feelings of despair and loneliness will once again overwhelm you.

Two years ago, my wife and I counseled a young lady who insisted she was the loneliest girl in the state of Texas. She said, "If I could only find a husband, get married, and settle down, I'd never be lonely again." We helped pray in her prince charming. She did get married to a fine young Christian gentleman. But three months after the wedding, she was back to us in tears, crying, "I'm still lonely. I'm still empty. I know now it wasn't just the man I needed. I haven't settled things in my own life yet." That girl will never be a good wife until she learns to quit leaning on other people to meet her needs.

A young divorcée asked my wife and me to pray that her estranged husband would return. She was nearly hysterical, crying, "I want him back so badly. I know I messed up our marriage—I was so crazy and immature. But now that he's gone, I want him back. I think I've grown up. I've matured. I know I can do it right this time, but he's been dating another woman. I'm so desperate that if God won't bring him back to me soon, I'm going to go out to the nearest bar and tag on the biggest drunk you ever saw."

I informed her we would not pray for his return, because she was not ready for him. She would mess it up all over again. Why? Because she was still not a whole person. She was ready to throw her morals away if he did not come home to try once again to make her happy. That is why many people don't get such prayers answered. They are not ready to try again. They would make the same mistakes all over again, even if remarried to someone else. They are still leaning on others, always using someone else as a crutch to hold them up. They have not become whole persons, and they are not complete in themselves.

God Alone Is the Only Source of All Happiness and Contentment

Paul said, ". . . my God shall supply all your need according to his riches in glory by Christ Jesus" (Philippians 4:19). Not your husband or your wife, pastor, psychiatrist, or your best friend—but God! Go ahead and share your problems with your friend or pastor or a professional counselor. But, in the final analysis, they can help you only if they make you face yourself. You must do it on your own—take your needs to the Lord and allow Him to make you whole. Eventually, you must get rid of every crutch and lean completely on Jesus alone.

When your relationship with the Lord is wrong, it affects all human relationships. Most Christian married couples are not having trouble with their marriages. Rather, they are having trouble with God, with faith, with prayer; therefore, they have trouble with each other.

When people confess to me that their marriages are in trouble, I don't have to dig too deeply until I discover they are not where they should be with the Lord. They are bored with the things of God, so they are bored with life and marriage. They have lost touch with God and, in turn, have lost touch with their spouses. These husbands and wives are not really suffering from a lack of communication with each other; they are suffering mostly from a lack of communication with God. When people quit talking to God, they quit talking to one another. And people who quit talking to God soon get very lonely and depressed. They are actually lonely for God, hungering for communion with Him, yearning for His close love and nearness; but, instead of recognizing these needs as spiritual, they blame their lack of fulfillment on their husbands or wives.

If most Christians were truly honest, they would have to admit there is nothing terminal about their marriage problems. What is wrong is their relationship to the Lord. Their faith is in trouble, and when people are not on right terms with God, they get frustrated and take it out on the ones they love the most. They are actually angry with themselves. That empty, restless feeling is a hunger for God. But instead of returning to the secret closet to satisfy that thirst, most Christians drift farther away and fall deeper into despair.

There is not a Christian in this world, who, deep in his heart, is not aware that God will help him. We know God can heal all our hurts; we know He can heal any marriage; we know He can wipe away every tear and bring joy. But we simply do not take the time or effort to run to Him in our hour of need.

You can be happy. You can be a whole person, and you need never again lean on another human being. That is not to say we don't need one another. We need the prayer, help, and comfort of loving friends and family. But there can be no lasting happiness if we expect others to create it for us.

Why not allow Him to renew your heart, renew a right spirit in you, and reveal to you that in His presence there is fullness of joy and pleasures evermore? That is why Jesus said, ". . . Be of good cheer. . . . Lo, I am with you alway . . ." (Matthew 14:27; 28:20).

4

Have You Felt Like Giving Up Lately?

A growing number of ministers have been writing to me, in recent months, telling of their concern for parishioners who are simply giving up. One minister wrote:

> I see my church members trying so hard to cope with problems in their marriages and pressures in their personal lives. Just when it seems victory is within reach, they stumble and fall. Good, honest Christians are so often overwhelmed by guilt and condemnation; it causes despair. When they can't live up to their own expectations, when they fall back into sin and get involved, they decide to give up. Few know how to pull out of a moral tailspin.

I agree with the assessment of these ministers. Growing numbers of Christians *are* at the breaking point. None of the talk about giving up has to do with the Lord. Few Christians would even dare entertain thoughts of quitting on their love for Jesus. Most despairing Christians think only of giving up on themselves. You hear it so often, "I just can't go on anymore. I can't make it, even though I try so hard. It's hopeless. Why try?"

I hear some ministers today who continually preach only a positive message. To hear them tell it, every Christian is receiving miracles; everybody is getting instant answers to prayer; everybody is feeling good, living good, and the whole world is bright and rosy. I love to hear that kind of preaching, because I really desire all those good and healthy things for God's people. But that's not the way things are for a great number of very honest, sincere Christians. How sad to hear such shallow theology being pushed from pulpits today. It's an insult to a lowly Jesus who became poor, who died a failure in the eyes of the world. It is this kind of materialistic preaching that has so ill prepared an entire generation to endure any kind of pain, to be content with such things as they have, to be abased and not always abounding. Serving God becomes a kind of Olympic race, in which everyone must strive for the gold medals.

No wonder our young people give up in defeat. They can't live up to the image, created by religion, of a happy-go-lucky, rich, successful, always positive-thinking Christian. Their world is not that idealistic. They look in a mirror reflecting a face covered with ugly pimples. They live with heartbreaks, hour-by-hour crises, and horrible family problems. Their friends are hooked and dying on all sides. They look into the uncertain future, frightened and worried. Loneliness, fear, and depression hound them daily.

Positive thinking won't make their problems go away. Confessing these problems don't really exist doesn't change a thing. These apostles of the positive dare not exclude the Gethsemane experiences of life. The cup of pain, the hour of isolation, and the night of confusion were all part of the Master's life-style. Our great achievements and our successes ought to take place at Gethsemane, not Fort Knox.

The sawdust trail for many has become the gold-dust trail.

The Bible has become a catalog, with unlimited order blanks for life's goodies for everyone who wants to become a "silver" saint. Anything having to do with Job-like pain and suffering is considered negative living.

God is good, and those who give generously do receive abundant blessings. One should always think on good and honest reports; but pain, poverty, and suffering have befallen some of the saintliest of God's people, just as they did righteous Job.

What do you say to that wife whose home is breaking up, while she seems powerless to stop it? She's been advised by her friends, counseled by her pastor, and exhorted over and over again, "Stay on your knees and believe God for a miracle." So she fasts, and she prays. She bends over backwards to the point of crawling on her knees to her husband. She exercises faith with every intellectual insight she possesses. But, in spite of all her honest efforts, he grows hard and bitter, demanding a divorce. Not all marriages are healed through prayer or good intentions. It takes two to make a marriage work, and even though prayer may bring the power of Holy Ghost conviction upon a straying mate, that mate can resist all of God's efforts and abort the solution.

Some of my friends may be wondering why I am spending so much time talking about marriage, divorce, and the home. The reason is simple enough: In my crusades I talk to so many kids on the brink of suicide, and an overwhelming majority tell me their depression stems from trouble at home. Dad and Mom are having trouble, or they have already gotten a divorce.

Multitudes of husbands and wives are giving up on their marriages. A minister friend of mine, whose divorce had just become final, told me he has become a hero of sorts to some of his closest friends. One friend called him and asked, "Where did you get the courage to split up? Man, we're having trouble, too, but I guess I'm a coward. Wish I could take that step."

Another called, saying, "Our marriage is a farce. We don't communicate at all anymore. I've given up. But how do you take that final plunge into divorce? I'm so hung up on security and my job; I'm just afraid I'd lose too much."

Still another called and offered, "I admire your courage. You got out of a hopeless situation. I guess I'll go on existing, living in misery. I don't want my kids to turn on me; that's the only thing holding me. I've given up completely on our marriage."

There are many of you who, at this very moment, are on the verge of giving up. You can't understand what is happening to you, to your marriage, to your home. Something is missing; and, try as you will, you simply cannot find the key to make things work out right. How many hours have you spent all alone, trying to figure out where things went wrong? The magic is gone. The romance is gone. The communication is gone. In their places now are arguments, questions, suspicions, innuendoes, cutting remarks.

A brokenhearted lady wrote:

> Sir, I just can't believe it's happening to me. I was so secure, feeling sorry for all those others who seemed to be having so many problems. Never did I imagine our marriage could crumble. I was too intelligent, too much into giving and sharing. Now I'm a victim of this curse of divorce. It's a shattering experience.

A successful marriage counselor took me to lunch recently and before the entree was served, he confessed his own marriage had been in jeopardy. "You just can't take any good marriage for granted anymore," he said. "I find I have to work harder than ever to keep a good thing. I'm convinced Satan is determined to break up my marriage and every good Christian marriage. It's a well-planned attack on the best of marriages. If Satan can get the strongest, most-admired marriages broken up, the weaker ones will be tempted to quit struggling and give up."

The secret struggles in the Christian's personal life are just as critical. The inner battles of the average Christian today are staggering in intensity and proportion. Multitudes are involved in situations too hard to comprehend. Like David, the Psalmist, they confessed, "My sins have overwhelmed me; they are too high for me to understand."

Paul said, "For we that are in this tabernacle do groan, being burdened . . ." (2 Corinthians 5:4). I doubt we could even count the great numbers of Christians who groan in secret, because of the burdens they carry.

Paul talked about trouble: ". . . trouble which came to us . . . we were pressed out of [burdened beyond] measure, above strength, insomuch that we despaired even of life" (2 Corinthians 1:8).

If you pulled back the facade from every great preacher and every admired personality, you would find moments of deep depression. You would find the same infirmities you find in any normal Christian. We all have seasons of despair, accompanied by feelings of failure. At times we have all thought of quitting. We have all had thoughts of giving up.

Why Do We Feel This Way?

Why do we feel like giving up at times? Mostly because we act as if God has forsaken the earth. We don't doubt His existence or His reality, but our prayers seem to go unanswered. We cry out for His help, in such desperation, and He seems not to hear. We struggle along, making one mistake after another. We make promises to do better; we get into the Bible; we cry and pray and stay busy helping others and doing good. But we are so often left with an empty, unfulfilled sensation. The promises of God haunt us. We claim those promises in what we believe is honest, childlike faith, but time after time we fail to receive what we ask for. In the hour of temptation, down we go!

Doubt creeps in, and Satan whispers, "Nothing works. Faith in God doesn't produce results. In spite of your tears, prayers, and trust in God's Word, nothing really changes. Days, weeks, and even years go by, and your prayers, hopes, and dreams are still unanswered and unfulfilled. Quit! Give up!"

Every Christian on this planet reaches that crisis point at one time or another in life. And in that moment, when the walls seem to be caving in and the roof appears to be collapsing, when everything seems to be coming apart and sin demands the upper hand, a voice deep within cries out, "Walk away from it all. Pack it in! Escape! Why put up with it? Run away. You don't have to take it. Do something drastic."

David, overwhelmed by the evil in his heart, cried out:

Awake, why sleepest thou, O Lord? arise, cast us not off for ever. Wherefore hidest thou thy face, and forgettest our affliction and our oppression?

Psalms 44:23, 24

Christian, does it amaze you that great men of God faced the same battles you and I face today? The Bible says:

Beloved, think it not strange concerning the fiery trial which is to try you, as though some strange thing happened unto you: But rejoice, inasmuch as ye are partakers of Christ's sufferings; that, when his glory shall be revealed, ye may be glad also with exceeding joy.

1 Peter 4:12, 13

Job was a perfect man, in God's sight; yet he, too, experienced a time when he wanted to give up. Job's agony came from a terrible dilemma. He was convinced, in his heart, that God knew where he was and what he was going through; yet he could not enter into the presence of God. He lamented:

> Behold, I go forward, but he is not there; and backward, but I cannot perceive him: On the left hand, where he doth work, but I cannot behold him: he hideth himself on the right hand, that I cannot see him.
>
> Job 23:8, 9

Job was saying to himself, "I know God is there someplace, looking down on me in all my trouble. He knows the way I take; but, in spite of all I do to find Him, He keeps hiding from me. I believe God is real; He is there; but I just can't see Him." In total desperation, Job sobs: ". . . I am afraid of him. . . . The Almighty troubleth me" (Job 23:15, 16).

All those fearful and troubled thoughts about God were the result of what Job thought was a divine do-nothingness. Job argues that God doesn't cut him off, yet He doesn't remove the darkness (*see* Job 23:17).

The bottom line for Job was simply this: Either cut me down or make things right; just don't be silent toward me. Even if You cut me off, at least I'll know You are there.

What Is the Cure?

How can we learn to hold on and live one day at a time? You can begin by forgetting all shortcuts and magic cures. The Christian doesn't need a supposed demon of despair cast out, as if his going would make life easier. Nor will God come down and do our living for us. The tempter will not be destroyed until that day God casts him into prison. Satan will always be here, deceiving, accusing, and trying to rob every believer of his faith.

The longer I live for Christ, the more difficult it is for me to accept easy, cure-all solutions. In my own struggles I've found great comfort and help in two wonderful absolutes.

God really loves me! This is the first absolute. God is not in the business of condemning His children—failures or not. He yearns over us as a loving Father, wanting only to lift us out of our weaknesses.

Recently I caught a glimpse of that love, while walking in the woods around our ranch. Not once did I stop to consider the birds flying about, free and healthy. But suddenly, there on the ground just ahead, flopped a crippled little bird. Struggling so hard to fly, the little baby bird could only flip over helplessly in the dust. I stooped to pick it up. It was then a familiar Scripture came flashing through my mind: ". . . and one [sparrow] . . . shall not fall on the ground without your Father" (Matthew 10:29).

I once thought that verse read, "Not a sparrow falls to the ground without the Father knowing about it." But Matthew's version states: "One shall not fall without the Father."

God is with us even when we fall. We do not fall without the Father. He does not fall into our sin, but He does come down to our fallen condition. He does not abandon us on our way down. He never forsakes a crippled child. For, you see, we are that sparrow.

David said, "I watch, and am as a sparrow alone upon the house top" (Psalms 102:7). David saw the bathing Bathsheba from that housetop, and he fell, a broken, crippled sparrow. But God did not give up on him. Our Lord never gives up on any of us.

Have you also fallen? Do you relate to that crippled sparrow, flopping helplessly in the dust? Are you wounded, hurting, and feeling lost and lonely? Do you ever think to yourself, "How can God put up with someone like me? How can He still love me when I've failed Him so badly"?

Oh, but He does love you, my friend. Often we can recognize His great love only when we have hit bottom and find ourselves in such need of it. You will have won a great victory if you can be convinced God loves you even in your wounded, crippled condition. It was a wound that made me kneel and show compassion for a helpless bird. And it is our wounds, our hurts, our helplessness which cause His love and compassion to overshadow and envelop us. Our strength is renewed by His everlasting love. Just rest in that wonderful love. Don't panic. Deliverance will come. God answers us by showing His love. When we have learned how weak we are and have learned to trust His love and forgiveness, He will stoop down and gently help us back to the nest.

It is my faith that pleases Him the most. The second absolute is this. ". . . without faith it is impossible to please him . . ." (Hebrews 11:6). ". . . Abraham believed God, and it was counted unto Him for righteousness."

God wants so much to be trusted. That trust He counts as righteousness. I know some very holy, sanctified people (at least outwardly) who walk the straight and narrow. They would never once admit to feelings of failure and despair. They think of themselves as saints; but their great sin is doubt. Sometimes I think certain sinners have more faith than many self-righteous Christians.

What do I do when temptation rolls over me like a flood? What do I do when my inadequacies overwhelm me, and I see the reflections of my weaknesses? Do I give up? Quit? Never! I bring to God all I have left: my faith in Him! I may not understand why He seems to take such a long time to intervene, but I know He will. He will keep His word to me.

I am convinced Satan wants to rob me of only one thing, and that is my faith. He really doesn't want my morals or my good deeds or my dreams. He wants to destroy my faith and make me believe God has forsaken this earth.

A fall is never fatal to those who keep their faith intact. In spite of continual struggles and feelings of helplessness, at times, I still believe my Lord. In spite of despair and pressures that stunt the mind and sap the strength, I believe God. I believe He will keep me from falling and present me faultless before the throne of glory, with exceeding great joy.

He loves me, and He wants me to keep on trusting; so I will accept that love, and keep my faith strong. "Thou wilt keep him in perfect peace, whose mind is stayed on thee: because he trusteth in thee" (Isaiah 26:3).

5

Are You Going Through

a Dry Spell?

I preach to thousands, yet there are times I feel so very dry, so far away from the warm presence of God. In these moments of dryness, I have no great yearning to read the Word; my reading of the Bible is done mostly through a sense of obligation. When I'm dry and empty, I feel little compulsion to pray. I know my faith is intact, and my love for Jesus is strong. There is no desire in me to taste the things of this world. It's just that I can't seem to touch God in those days and weeks of spiritual dryness.

Have you ever sat in church and watched those all around you getting blessed, while you feel nothing? They cry; they pray; they worship with tremendous feelings. But you are not moved upon at all. You begin to wonder if there is something wrong with your spiritual life. Christians all around you are telling great stories about how God is blessing them and answering all their prayers. They seem to live on a mountain-top of happy experiences, while you just plod along, loving Jesus but not setting the world on fire. Some of your prayers still have not been answered. You don't shout or put on an emotional display. You have no big stories to tell about some fantastic miracle you've witnessed. It almost makes you feel like a second-class believer.

I believe all true believers experience dry spells at various times in their Christian lives. Even Jesus felt the isolation when He cried aloud: "Father, why have you forsaken me?"

Notes From My Diary, During a Dry Spell

I keep notes of almost every thought I receive in my nighttime devotions. Recently, during a dry spell, I recorded my feelings. I think there are many Christians who will relate to these honest notations made in my diary.

A note of caution before reading this very personal confession: When I talk about the sin in my own life, do not try to interpret that as some hideous, openly flaunted weakness. To me, whatever is not of faith is sin. We have all sinned and fallen short of the glory of God. I often fall into the gross sin of doubt. So please do not read into my confession of sin something not intended. Think of your own sin as you read.

I wonder why God seems to be so distant at times. Is He angry with me? Does He have to hide from me because of failure in my life? Is God holding back on me in some way, bound by a contract in His Holy Word that demands He close His eyes in my direction, because of my stubbornness?

Does sin cause a separation? Is God really there, wanting to break through to me with overwhelming joy and peace, but unable to, because of a barrier I have constructed as a result of a besetting sin? Must He hide against His will because He honors His Word above His name? He hid from Israel in times of backsliding. Must He hide from me for a while, until I see the horror of my sins and run from them?

Does He finally get weary of my constant falling, and must He shut me off for a while only because He loves

me so? Does His omnipotent love demand He isolate me
from His presence, until I break and yield, as a submit-
ting child, weary of my emptiness and despair?

Or is all of this dryness a result of my own blindness?
Is it just a result of living on feelings? Is He there all the
time, in spite of my failure, waiting for me to accept His
forgiveness? Do I feel isolated only because I'm ashamed
and burdened with guilt? Do I shun Him because I know
I'm unworthy of His blessings? Has the knowledge of my
weaknesses made me believe I have no right to expect
this nearness and comfort?

I am not morbid; I have no death wish. It's not just the
nighttime blues. I never once doubt my eternal salvation.
What I do doubt is my ability to understand how God works. I
have always felt the power of His great love. Even in my
driest hours, the sense of His love for me is almost overwhelming. It is not enough to know the Father loves you; it is
not enough to believe all His promises; it is not enough to
walk in faith; it is not enough to know you want the Lord with
all that is in you. There must be more.

There must be the nearness of the Lord, the still small
voice and the joy of hearing that voice. There must be the
knowledge that He not only abides, but that His Word is even
in your mouth. The heart must feel His warmth. The flow of
God's presence must fill the room. The tears that are all bottled up inside must find release. The joy of Jesus must rush
through all the corridors of your mind. The heart must know
He has come to guide, comfort, and help in the hour of need.
There must be no doubt, no question that God has chosen to
come and commune with His servant.

Without the nearness of God, there can be no peace. The
dryness can be stopped only with the dew of His glory. The

despair can be dispelled only by the assurance God is answering. The fire of the Holy Ghost must heat the mind, body, and soul.

I want God's total presence. I want to flow in His river of love. I want complete forgiveness of all my sins, but more than forgiveness, I want freedom. What is forgiveness without freedom? I know the Lord has promised to forgive me seven times in a single day. I know His love and forgiveness are to all generations. I know if I confess my sins, He is faithful and just to forgive and to cleanse me. But it is not enough to be forgiven and cleansed from yesterday's sins. I need freedom from the power of the sin that so easily besets me, freedom from the slavery of all passions, freedom from the chains of all iniquity.

I know God's Word promises freedom. I know the many Scriptures which talk of walking in the Spirit to avoid fulfilling the lusts of the flesh. I know about the warnings to flee all lusts. Other Scriptures flood my mind about overcoming the world, but there are times I don't seem to find the key. How do these verses work in a practical way in my everyday life? What does it really mean to walk in the Spirit? Does that mean you will never fall again? A child keeps falling while learning to walk. Adults stumble and fall. Can you fall, even while walking in the Spirit, then get up and walk again, getting stronger as you go?

God, You've got to be there! If You are not there in my time of dryness, there is no hope. You must be there, calling for me, longing for my voice, yearning over me as a father pities his child. If not, life has no meaning.

He cannot give up on me when I'm hurting. Yes, my flesh is weak. Yes, I fail Him over and over again. Yes, I've told Him how sorry I am a thousand times a year. Yes, I've promised to forsake the world and everything in it, but, at times, I can't seem to keep my word. Yes, there are a few times I feel like

the worst kind of sinner, a cheat, a cad, a two-timing, worth-
less child. Yes, I do feel I am unworthy to ever expect Him to
come near me when I feel so cheap and ungrateful.

But, in spite of all that, somehow I know He is not far off.
Somehow I hear a distinct, small voice calling, "Come, My
child. I am aware of all you are experiencing. I still love you. I
will never leave you nor forsake you. We will face it together.
I am still your Father, and you are My child. Come, not on
your merits or goodness, but come on the merits of your
Saviour, Jesus the Lord."

Somehow I know He will bring me out of this dry spell. I
have in me a flame that will not be smothered. I seem to know
the promises will be fulfilled. In His time, in His way, He will
turn my dryness into a river of love. His Word will come to
me. I will receive a new revelation of His will, a renewed
spirit, and a greater peace of mind, all because He has never
failed me once before.

Oh, God! I have feet of clay. My mind is strong in faith. My
heart melts for You. My tears are hot with desire for the touch
of the Lord, but my feet keep taking me astray. I am not
walking in the Spirit, as I would honestly like to. Where is
that day-by-day victory? Where is the power to keep myself
holy and pure?

God, I search the Scripture, hoping to find a formula, a way
out of the bondage of sin. If it means staying on my knees all
night, then I'll do it. Does it mean reading my Bible through,
until I stumble on a clear message of deliverance? Then I'll
read and read! Most of the clichés and easy solutions offered
by preachers do not work, even though they sound pious.

Somewhere there has to be victory over all the power of the
enemy. Somewhere I can put aside the weight, the burden,
the harassment. God promises total freedom, total victory
over the power of the enemy. Someday my foot will no longer
be snared in Satan's trap. Someday I'll look into my heart and

see only Jesus, only holiness, only those things pleasing to God.

Someday God must lead all His children to a place of freedom from sin's power. The Word of God is so vast; I know so little of how to find in it the answers to my personal needs. The only hope is the Holy Spirit, who will supernaturally lead me to the truth that will set me free. I can't find it by myself. I can't get it out of books or from counselors. I can't understand any of it without the Holy Spirit revealing it to me. I want to know what God expects of me; I want to know how much is my part and how much is His!

Oh, God! Cleanse my desires. Make me desire those things You know to be best for me. If You gave me everything I desired, it would be a bedlam of confusion, with no order or harmony left. All my human desires are blind. They are usually out of keeping with my real needs and are often contrary to God's moral laws.

It is so easy to desire what would cause the greatest damage to myself, lead to the worst misery, and bring on the most tragic kind of confusion. I think of my desires as being well thought out, intelligent, and needful to my well-being.

Sin causes my desires to be loosed from God's moral law. They end up as foamings of the inner appetites. Soul hunger, aspirations, lusts, and passions reek with all kinds of disorder. They are phantoms without perception.

Where do many of my desires originate? Not from a spring of reason and common sense, but they are instigated, instead, by raw lustings of the old nature. They rush out of my mind like wild troops, confused, blind, and in total disarray. They swarm like bees, fast and wild.

As time goes by, I so often discover how vain and foolish my desires were. I desired to undertake a new project, and it exploded before I could get started. Later, I learned my disappointment was a blessing in disguise. If God had not interfered and kept those desires from me, I could have destroyed myself.

My desires can often be very morally bad. They can be fouled by lust. There is an entire breed of desires lurking beneath the surface, constantly pushed upon us all by our Adam nature, always breaking into the mind, mingling with our deepest and holiest thoughts. These evil desires seek to identify with our best thoughts, trying to make the mind accept them as God's thoughts.

Very often my personal desires are so dominant, so deeply imbedded, that they invade my mind in the secret closet. They become so powerful and persistent, I allow them to deceive me into accepting them as the still small voice of God in the inner man. May God keep me from the deception of my own immoral desires!

What Shall I Do to Overcome Spiritual Dryness?

I must maintain a life of prayer. Why is it none of us pray as we should, anymore? We know God is wanting to comfort and help us. We know our burdens can all be lifted when we are shut in with Him. There is something deep within us that keeps calling us to prayer. It is the voice of the Holy Spirit saying, "Come!" Come to the water that satisfies that soul thirst. Come to the Father, who pities His children. Come to the Lord of life, who promises to forgive every sin committed. Come to the One who refuses to condemn you or forsake you or hide from you.

God does not hide from us when we sin. Never! That is only our fear condemning our hearts. God did not hide in the garden, when Adam and Eve sinned. He still came to them, calling and yearning for their fellowship and love. We, ourselves, hide because of our guilt and condemnation. We can't imagine God still loving us when we are so disobedient and ungrateful.

Come boldly to His throne of grace, even when you have sinned and failed. He instantly forgives those who repent with godly sorrow. You don't have to spend hours and days in remorse and guilt. You don't have to earn your way back into His good graces. You don't have to pretend a superficial kind of sorrow or feign tears. Go to the Father, bend your knees, open your heart, and cry out your agony and pain. Tell Him all about your failings, all about your struggles. Tell Him about your loneliness, feelings of isolation, fears, and failures.

We try everything except prayer. We read books, looking for formulas and guidelines. We go to friends, ministers, and counselors, looking everywhere for a word of comfort or advice. We seek mediators and forget the one Mediator who has the answer to everything.

We don't pray, because it's so hard to do—most of the time. It's not hard when trouble comes unexpectedly, or when cancer strikes, or when a loved one suddenly dies of a heart attack. At these times we are so broken in spirit that we cry and pray. That's all right, but we should be leaning on Jesus through the good and the bad. We should be getting our strength and help long before the crisis overwhelms us. We should be pouring out our hearts to Him, every day of our lives.

No wonder we are so dry and empty. We have simply neglected the secret closet of prayer. It is not really dryness; it is lukewarmness. It is a growing coldness, caused by drifting along, getting away from the holy place.

Nothing dispels dryness and emptiness more quickly than an hour or two shut in with God. Putting off that date with God in His secret closet causes guilt. We know our love for Him should lead us into His presence; but we busy ourselves in so many other things, then time slips away, and God is left out. We throw in His direction a whole array of "thought prayers." But nothing can take the place of that secret closet with the door shut, praying to the Father in that seclusion. That is the solution to every dry spell.

I must no longer be afraid of a little suffering. Christ's Resurection was preceded by a short period of suffering. We do die! We do suffer! There is pain and sorrow!

We do not want to suffer or resist or be hurt. We want painless deliverance. We want supernatural intervention. "Do it, God," we pray, "because I am weak and always will be. Do it all while I go my way, waiting for a supernatural deliverance." Or we blame our troubles on demons! We seek out a man of God and hope he can cast the demon out, so we can go our way with no pain or suffering. All done! Breeze right through to a peaceful life of victory. We want someone to lay hands on us and drive away all the dryness. But victory is not always without suffering and pain. Look at your sin. Face it. Suffer it through, as Jesus did. Fill up His suffering. Enter into it. Suffering endures only for a night, but joy always follows in the morning.

God sets before you a choice. His love demands a choice. If God supernaturally lifted us out of every battle, without pain or suffering, it would abort all trials and all temptation; there would be no free choice and no testing as by fire. It would be God superimposing His will on mankind. He chooses to meet us in our dryness and show us how it can become the way into a new life of faith.

It is often according to the will of God to suffer dryness and even pain: "Wherefore let them that suffer according to the will of God commit the keeping of their souls to him in well doing, as unto a faithful Creator" (1 Peter 4:19).

Thank God, suffering is always the short period before final victory! "But the God of all grace, who hath called us unto his eternal glory by Christ Jesus, after that ye have suffered a while, make you perfect, stablish, strengthen, settle you" (1 Peter 5:10).

6

Victory Over Your Besetting Sin

Sin causes Christians to become craven cowards who live in humiliating defeat. They can't stand up, with courage, against sin, because of the secret sin in their own lives. They excuse the sins of others, because of the disobedience in their own hearts; and they can't preach victory, because they live in defeat. Some of them once knew what it was like to live victoriously, taking vengeance against sin, having fulfilled Christ's righteousness in their own lives. They experienced the power, the courage, and the blessings, that come to those who are obedient to the Lord. Today they are but a shadow of their former selves. They hang their heads in shame, unable to look the world in the eye, victimized by a sin that rules their lives. A besetting sin has robbed them of their spiritual vitality, and one enemy after another is raised up against them.

A once mightily used evangelist now sells cars in a small town in Texas. He stood in the pulpit as a powerful preacher of the Gospel, and thousands were converted through his ministry. He became an adulterer, left his wife, and ran off with his girl friend. In just a few weeks, he lost everything. That minister is now but a shell of his old self. To see him shuffle about, beaten down and sad eyed, is pitiful. He lives in constant fear and spends sleepless nights thinking of what

could have been. His anxieties have made him physically ill;
he has chest pains, ulcers, and hypertension. He has repented
of his sin, but he cannot undo the past. God forgives, but
people don't!

A sixteen-year-old youth confessed to me: "I'm having sex
with my girl friend. I've been reading what the Bible says
about fornication and adultery, and now I'm scared. I worry
that God will have to judge me, if the Bible is true. I keep
doing it, and I'm full of fear, guilt, and worry. It seems as
though there are two people inside of me, a good person and a
bad person. I am afraid the bad person in me will overpower
the good person, and God will have to give up on me. How
can I make sure the good person in me gets the victory?"

Both the minister and the boy have been overpowered by
their enemies of guilt, fear, and depression. They are victims,
defeated and humiliated by unseen enemies that threaten to
destroy them. Sin always brings on the enemies. Sin weakens
all resistance; it turns warriors into weaklings. Lust conceives,
then it brings on sin, and sin brings on the enemy to destroy.

We Must Learn From Examples in the Old Testament

David had enemies. They were the Philistines, the Amo-
rites, the Ammonites, the Syrians, and other various enemies
arrayed against Israel. When David was right with the Lord
and in good fellowship, none of his enemies could stand before him. He slew them by the tens of thousands, and his
name was feared in every enemy camp. But when David
sinned and became estranged from the Lord, his enemies
grew bold and triumphed over him. Sin caused him to lose his
courage and confidence, making him weak before all his
enemies.

David's sin of adultery immediately followed one of his
greatest victories. The Ammonite-Syrian war was one of Is-

rael's greatest battles. David gathered all Israel together, passed with them over Jordan, and did battle at Helam. The Syrians fled before Israel; seven hundred chariots were destroyed, forty thousand horsemen were killed, and all the kings allied to the Ammonites and Syrians fled. The chapter on this great war closes by saying, ". . . they made peace with Israel, and served them . . ." (2 Samuel 10:19).

This great man of God, basking in the glory of his greatest victory, began to lust after Bathsheba, killed her husband Uriah, and committed adultery with her. ". . . But the thing that David had done displeased the Lord" (2 Samuel 11:27).

So the Lord sent the Prophet Nathan to David. The prophet did not come with a message of love and understanding. He did not come to counsel David on how to handle his guilt and condemnation. He did not offer the king a salve for his stricken conscience. Rather, Nathan got right to the heart of the matter. "You are the man. You have despised the commandment of the Lord. You have done evil in the sight of the Lord. You are guilty of secret sin" (*see* 2 Samuel 12:7–9).

Sin Brings on Its Own Judgment

To a man after His own heart, God had to say, ". . . Behold, I will raise up evil against thee out of thine own house . . ." (2 Samuel 12:11). Shortly after, his beloved son Absalom turned against him, and David fled for his life into the wilderness. What a pitiful sight!

> And David went up by the ascent of mount Olivet, and wept as he went up, and had his head covered, and he went barefoot: and all the people that was with him covered every man his head, and they went up, weeping as they went up.
>
> 2 Samuel 15:30

Is this weeping, barefoot, broken man the same great king who, just months before, had defeated two world powers?

What turned him into a weak, powerless, cowardly man who fled before the enemy? It was sin—nothing else! Like Samson, David was shorn of his courage and power, because he caved in to the weakness of his flesh.

Solomon, too, was feared by all his enemies. Pharaoh's armies were held off by his powerful reputation. The Edomites dared not attack so powerful a king. His was a glorious reign, and his fame was unparalleled. He was blessed, prospered, and honored in everything he did. But Solomon sinned against the Lord and permitted his love for God to grow cold. He lost touch with heaven. And look what happened. God said to him, "Because you failed to keep my covenant and my statutes and have turned aside to other gods, I will rend the kingdom from you" (*see* 1 Kings 11:9–11).

Suddenly the enemies of Solomon fell upon him. "And the Lord stirred up an adversary unto Solomon, Hadad the Edomite . . ." (1 Kings 11:14). Not just one enemy, but two: "And God stirred him up another adversary, Rezon . . . and he abhorred Israel . . ." (1 Kings 11:23, 25).

Sin and compromise so weakened this mighty king that even his servant became an enemy. "And Jeroboam . . . Solomon's servant . . . even he lifted up his hand against the king" (1 Kings 11:26).

Not a single enemy of Israel could stand before her when that nation did what was right before God. Israel's enemies fled in terror at the mention of her name. The enemies' hearts melted like wax when the victorious armies of Israel went to war, with banners waving. But when Israel sinned, even her weakest enemies prevailed against her. Achan committed an accursed sin, and the minuscule army of Ai sent Israel running in humiliation and defeat.

Listen to the prayer of Solomon at the dedication of the temple, and you soon discover all Israel was very much aware of what made the nation victorious and what brought defeat upon the people: